KT-226-315

HEALTH CHOICES

EXERCISE AND PLAY

Cath Senker

HODDER
Wayland

An imprint of Hodder Children's Books

Text copyright © Cath Senker 2004

Consultant: Jayne Wright
Design: Sarah Borny

Published in Great Britain in 2004
by Hodder Wayland, an imprint of
Hodder Children's Books

The right of Cath Senker to be identified as the author of this Work has
been asserted by her in accordance with the Copyright, Designs and Patents Act 1988

All rights reserved. No part of this publication may be reproduced,
stored in a retrieval system, or transmitted, in any form or by any means without
the prior permission of the publisher, nor be otherwise circulated in any form of binding
or cover other than that in which it is published and without a similar condition
being imposed on the subsequent purchaser.

The publishers would like to thank the following for allowing
us to reproduce their pictures in this book:
Corbis; 5, 18, 19, 21 / Hodder Wayland Picture Library;
4, 6, 7, 8, 9, 10, 11, 12, 13, 14, 15, 16, 17, 20

A catalogue record for this book is available from the British Library.

ISBN 07502 45018

Printed in China by WKT

Hodder Children's Books
A division of Hodder Headline Limited
338 Euston Road, London NW1 3BH

Contents

Why do I need to be active?

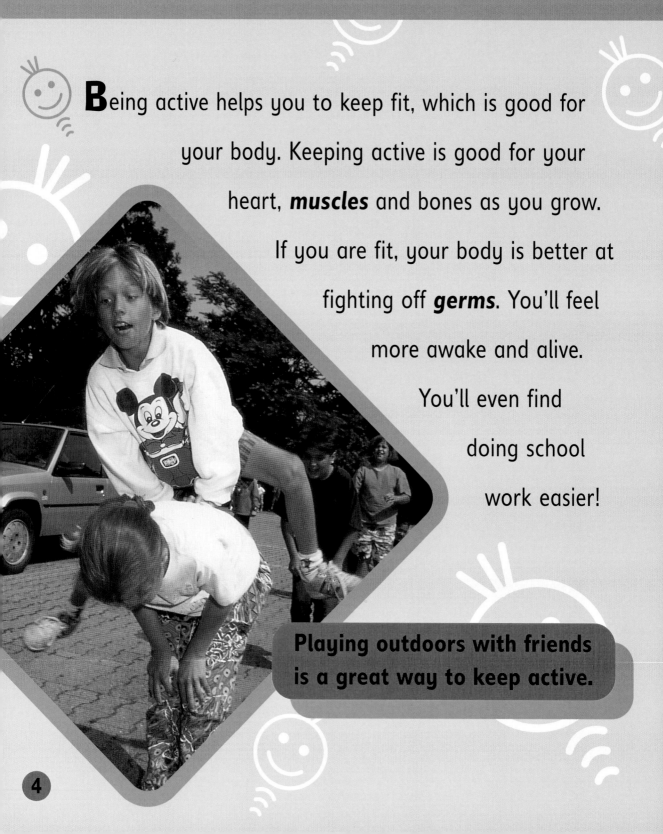

Being active helps you to keep fit, which is good for your body. Keeping active is good for your heart, **muscles** and bones as you grow. If you are fit, your body is better at fighting off **germs**. You'll feel more awake and alive. You'll even find doing school work easier!

Playing outdoors with friends is a great way to keep active.

This boy is doing Tae Kwon Do. Which sports have you tried? What else would you like to try?

It is best to be active for at least one hour every day.

There are so many activities and sports to choose from.

Walking, skipping, cycling and swimming are great

activities. For sport, have you tried football, tennis,

rounders or **badminton**? Don't just sit – keep fit!

What happens when I exercise?

You get out of breath, feel warmer and your heart beats faster. You feel full of life, and it's a great feeling.

When you exercise, your heart works harder pumping blood around your body. This makes you feel warm. Your muscles need more **oxygen** so you have to breathe harder. This is why you feel out of breath.

Ask an adult to show you how to take your **pulse**. How many beats per minute is your pulse rate? It's time to start working your heart! Run on the spot for five minutes. Then take your pulse. How fast is your pulse now you have worked your heart?

Can you describe how you feel after you have done some exercise?

What happens if you're not active?

People are more likely to put on weight if they do not stay fit and active. This extra weight puts a **strain** on the heart. It can make people very unwell.

It's fun to watch television but better not to watch it for a long time.

Children who are inactive may grow up to be unhealthy. They might get fat if they also eat a bad *diet*. They will get out of breath easily and will often feel tired.

It's a good idea to play quiet games to calm down after running around.

We can't stay active for every second of the day.

After running around, some rest is best! Life is about

doing a mixture of activities.

What can I do at playtime?

It's playtime – hooray! Which games do you play? Learn to skip with a skipping rope – see how many skips you can do. Perhaps you have a hopscotch game marked on the ground. You could play chase – or have a race.

What's your favourite playground game?

Have you ever played 'duck duck goose'? Stand in a circle. Go round the circle, saying 'duck' to each person. Then say 'goose' to one person. That person has to chase you back to their place. If they catch you, you're out!

Ask some adults what games they played as children. Maybe you could try them out.

Why is cycling good for me?

Cycling makes you out of breath so it is good for your heart. It helps you to develop strong legs and improve your balance. You can ride a scooter or skateboard to keep active too.

Cycling is good if it's safe. Remember – always wear a helmet. Your head is delicate. A helmet will protect your head if you fall off. Get some wheels – see how great it feels!

Wear bright colours when you are cycling and skating so that drivers and other people can see you.

Where do you like to ride your bike? It's best to use a quiet cycle path or go to the park. Perhaps you can cycle, scoot or skate to school if there is a safe *route*.

Is swimming good exercise?

Going to the pool is really cool. Swimming is good for your whole body. It's one of the best kinds of exercise you can do.

Keep afloat with armbands or a float. Practise kicking your legs and pulling through the water with your arms. Swim on your front and your back – you'll soon get the knack. Remember to keep breathing steadily.

How many different ways can you travel through water?
You can go really fast on a water slide!

It's important to learn to swim to be safe near water at the swimming pool, ponds, lakes, rivers and the sea. Take care, and you won't fall in. If you do, though, you can keep afloat until someone rescues you.

What can I learn in PE?

In PE you learn to move your body in different ways. You can learn to balance. Can you walk along a bench without falling off? Climbing on the apparatus helps you to **co-ordinate** your movements.

On the floor you can do more. See how many different ways you can travel forwards, backwards and sideways. Use a mat for forward and backward rolls. Can you do the crab position? Try doing handstands and cartwheels with your legs high in the air.

How many ways can you throw and catch a ball?

That's not all – there

are games with a ball.

You can play throw and catch, or hit the ball with a bat.

Is dancing just for girls?

No! It's for girls and boys. Dancing helps your body to become strong and develops your co-ordination. Using dance, you can show different ideas and moods. Listen to some music. How does it make you feel? Can you control your body carefully as you move?

Girls can play football too.

You can set up a game of football almost anywhere.

All you need is some space, a ball, and lots of energy.

It's a great game for developing teamwork and **tactics**.

Work out how your team can keep the ball. Move it

to the best place to score a goal!

What can I do at the park?

You can get all the exercise you need in the park. Maybe you have a playground near your home.

Can you swing along the monkey bars like a monkey swings through the trees? This develops strength in your arms. Playing on a swing is just the thing for making your legs strong.

Going on the climbing frame helps to keep your body *flexible*. You will improve your balance too.

There is plenty of space to run about. Bring a ball for throwing and catching games. When you go to the park, you'll want to stay till it's dark!

Glossary and index

strain	8	Harm to a part of the body because it has to work too hard.
tactics	19	The methods you use to do something.

Finding out more

Books to read:
Staying Safe on Bikes
by Maribeth Boelts,
(Franklin Watts, 1998)

For Key Stage 2
Gymnastics, Soccer,
Martial Arts, Volleyball,
all by Bernie Blackall
(Heinemann Library, 1998)